CHOOSE
CALM

A JOURNAL FOR HEALING ANXIETY, BREATHING IN, AND LETTING GO

NADIA HAYES

CASTLE POINT BOOKS
NEW YORK

www.stmartins.com
www.castlepointbooks.com

The Castle Point Books trademark is owned
by Castle Point Publishing, LLC.
Castle Point books are published and distributed
by St. Martin's Press.

ISBN 978-1-250-20022-8 (trade paperback)

Our books may be purchased in bulk for promotional, educational,
or business use. Please contact your local bookseller or the
Macmillan Corporate and Premium Sales Department at
1-800-221-7945, extension 5442, or by email
at MacmillanSpecialMarkets@macmillan.com.

First Edition: November 2018

10 9 8 7 6 5 4 3 2 1

THIS BOOK BELONGS TO:

INTRODUCTION

Anxiety is the worry that never ceases to unravel, the apprehension that takes hold when entering a new situation, and the feeling of discomfort that leads to a mild current of panic. It isn't until we understand anxiety as a lack of confidence in ourselves that we can begin to grapple with it, pin it down, and declare victory over it. Take aim at your own anxiety as you journey through the pages of *Choose Calm.* Inside you'll find a variety of exercises, prompts, and creative strategies for confronting everyday anxiety and freeing yourself from its tight grip. Find the calming methods that work for you and stop to use them whenever you need comfort. Share the exercises in this book with others who are working toward the same goal. Revel in the fact that people can change how they think. Over time, with small daily reminders to help them let go, anyone can lift the weight of anxiety. Feeling calm, centered, and relaxed isn't just something to wish for; it's a choice to be made. Make it today and every day.

IDENTIFY THE GREATEST SOURCES OF CALM AND COMFORT IN YOUR LIFE.

Maybe they include a blanket, a song, a friend, a pet, or a hobby. List all of the things you do to feel more at peace in the banners below.

warm Blanket

~ a Hug ~

Walk outside

~ prayer ~

Being / Relaxing w/ Family & Friends

~ Trying to Meditate ~

~ a Nap ~

There are
no riches like
the sweetness
of content.

We need to be content *

—R. CHAMBERLAIN

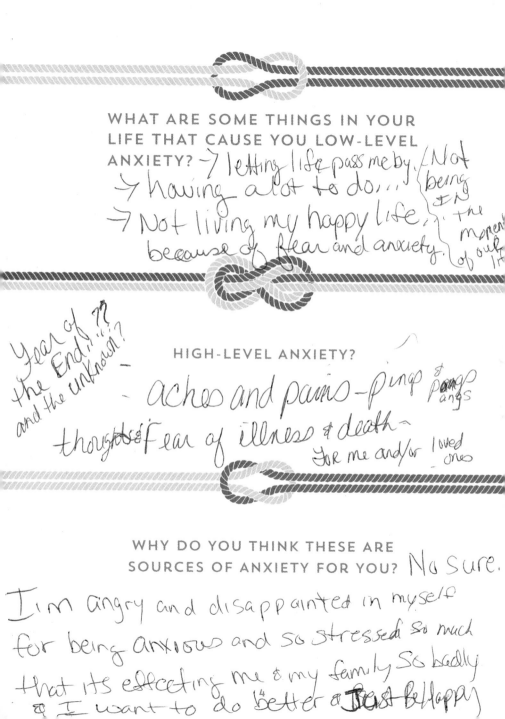

WHAT ARE SOME THINGS IN YOUR LIFE THAT CAUSE YOU LOW-LEVEL ANXIETY?

→ letting life pass me by. (Not
→ having alot to do... (being
→ Not living my happy life, In the
because of fear and anxiety. moment
of our li

HIGH-LEVEL ANXIETY?

Fear of ?? the End!!!? and the unknown?

- aches and pains - pings & pangs
thoughts & Fear of illness & death -
For me and/or loved ones

WHY DO YOU THINK THESE ARE SOURCES OF ANXIETY FOR YOU?

No sure.

I'm angry and disappointed in myself
for being anxious and so stressed so much
that its effecting me & my family so badly
& I want to do better & Just be Happy

Notice how you feel today and give it a name below.

How would family members, friends, and coworkers describe your mood today?

_____

_____

_____

_____

_____

WE MUST FREE
OURSELVES OF THE
HOPE THAT THE SEA
WILL EVER REST.
WE MUST LEARN TO
SAIL IN HIGH WINDS.

—ARISTOTLE ONASSIS

HOW WOULD YOU DRAW ANXIETY IF YOU HAD TO? Would it be a swirling tornado, a growling beast, or a train off its track? Try sketching your creative interpretation of anxiety below.

DON'T EVER BE AFRAID TO FOLLOW A SMALL BUT NAGGING WORRY TO ITS END. Anxiety can trick us into believing that we are headed for absolute disaster when the reality is much less foreboding.

Imagine that something you are worried about actually happens. What is the most likely outcome and how would you deal with it? Write it in the crystal ball.

I hope for
NOTHING.
I fear
NOTHING.
I am
FREE.

—NIKOS KAZANTZAKIS

Describe one strategy you have for battling anxiety and how effective it is.

STRATEGY:

WHEN I USE IT:

Rate how well it works on a scale of 1 (not that well) to 10 (perfectly well):

1   2   3   4   5   6   7   8   9   10

CALMNESS

IS THE CRADLE
OF POWER.

—JOSIAH GILBERT HOLLAND

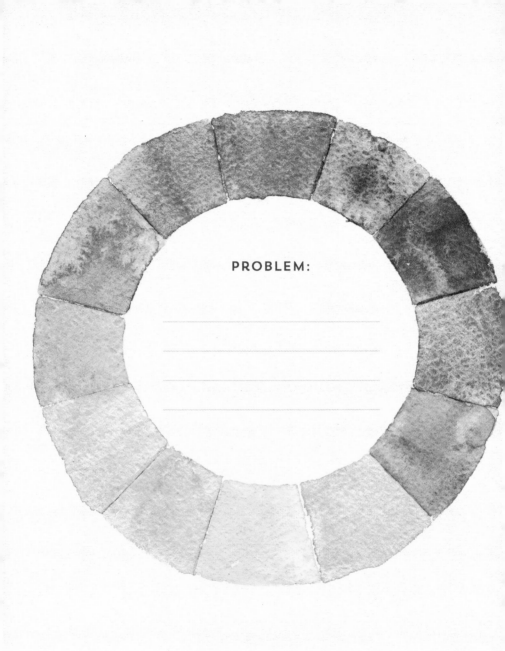

PROBLEM:

_____

_____

_____

_____

DESCRIBE ONE SITUATION OR PROBLEM IN THE CENTER OF THIS RAINBOW WHEEL. Imagine that each separate block of color is a unique perspective on this situation. How would your best friend phrase the situation? How would your mother advise you? Write the names of different people in each colored segment and consider how they might approach the problem. Which perspective feels the healthiest or the best? Try it on for size.

Describe a brighter view of the situation here:

WHAT MEMORIES CAN YOU ESCAPE
TO WHEN REALITY FEELS LIKE IT'S
BOXING YOU IN? Visualize a carefree childhood
moment or a peaceful spot you've visited in the past.
Maybe it's the day you got your first pet; maybe it's the
summers spent at your favorite relative's house; maybe
it's just a glimpse of your last vacation.

Describe it here in full sensory detail:

_____

_____

_____

_____

_____

_____

_____

_____

_____

_____

Revisit this memory in a frenzied moment, paint a
picture in your mind until you feel calm, and use it as a
tool for finding contentment.

WHAT STRUGGLES HAVE YOU SURVIVED? They can be small (losing your wallet) or big (losing your job). Write them down on the badges below to remember that you are a survivor. Anytime you feel uncertain as to whether you can handle what's coming, return to this list of accomplishments. Remember that you have the strength to get through anything.

DON'T LET A WORRY TRICK YOU INTO THINKING IT'S LARGER THAN IT IS. IT'S NOTHING BUT A DROP. In the grand scheme of your life, it is one small molecule. In a few days, or weeks, or months, the waves of your life experience will wash over it and it will disappear beneath the surface.

Imagine that the space below is a vast ocean representing the scope of your life experiences. Draw a tiny dot to represent today's greatest worry/problem. Relax as you add shades of deep blue to cover over it. Imagine a day when it won't matter much at all.

This, too, shall pass.

WORRYING DOESN'T
EMPTY TOMORROW
OF ITS SORROW,
IT EMPTIES TODAY
OF ITS STRENGTH.
EVERYTHING YOU HAVE
EVER WANTED, IS
SITTING ON THE OTHER
SIDE OF FEAR.

– GEORGE ADDAIR

THERE ARE SOME OF US WHO, AT THE END OF THE DAY, TEND TO REHASH THE NEGATIVE AND FORGET THE POSITIVE. Change the balance of your thoughts today. Vent all the negatives of your day below, but balance them out by writing twice as many positives. If this habit doesn't come automatically, then practice it until it does.

NEGATIVES
FROM TODAY

POSITIVES
FROM TODAY

SOME OF US THINK
HOLDING ON MAKES
US STRONG;

but sometimes it
is letting go.

—HERMANN HESSE

WHAT EXPECTATIONS DO YOU HAVE FOR YOURSELF? Circle your level of expectations in each area below.

Expectations for Myself as a Worker

LOW   MEDIUM   HIGH

Expectations for Myself as a Daughter/Son/Sister/Brother

LOW   MEDIUM   HIGH

Expectations for Myself as a Parent

LOW   MEDIUM   HIGH

Expectations for Myself as a Partner

LOW   MEDIUM   HIGH

Are you putting an intense amount of pressure on yourself in one or more specific areas? Describe why you think that is and how you might ease up and provide more realistic expectations for yourself.

GENTLE AND REPETITIVE MOTION OR SOOTHING ACTIVITIES ARE USEFUL TOOLS ON ANXIOUS DAYS. Spend a little quality time on a glider, a swing, or a rocking chair and indulge in soothing your inner child. Check off any motion activities below that would soothe you.

☐ ROCKING IN A ROCKING CHAIR

☐ SWINGING ON A SWING

☐ SITTING IN A GLIDER

☐ LYING IN A HAMMOCK

How might you add some of these motion activities to your day to bring yourself peace?

_____

_____

_____

_____

_____

WE RARELY PAUSE TO TAKE NOTICE OF OUR BREATH. Spend more time considering how quickly and deeply you are breathing. When you're feeling calm and centered, count how many breaths you take in one minute.

RECORD THAT NUMBER HERE:

The next time you are worried or stressed, count the number of breaths you take in a minute.

RECORD IT HERE:

In a harried moment, take time to count your breaths as a way to gauge your level of stress. Focus on your breath until it naturally slows. Sit in stillness, darkness, or roam away from the source of your stress if it helps.

Peace

IS LIBERTY IN TRANQUILITY.

—MARCUS TULLIUS CICERO

PATIENCE IS A LOST ART FOR MOST OF US. If you find yourself squirming anxiously behind the wheel while sitting in traffic, or tapping your foot irritably in line, take a moment to acknowledge and name this feeling of impatience. Instead of trying to push time forward, follow its easy tempo. Settle into the moment, no matter how uncomfortable it may feel at first.

TRY THESE TECHNIQUES TO HELP YOU WAIT MORE COMFORTABLY:

+ Remind yourself to breathe deeply and release control over the situation.

+ Stretch or do tiny foot flexes, neck rolls, or any other exercise that feels good in the moment.

+ Picture time not as an hourglass running out of sand, but as a vast desert with millions of grains of sand laid out before you.

WHEN I LET GO
OF WHAT I AM,
I BECOME WHAT
I MIGHT BE.

- LAO TZU

WHAT DO YOU BELIEVE IS WRITTEN IN YOUR STARS? Think of some things that you are destined to do or become and write them below. How can you make sure that these fated milestones don't pass you by?

What are some things you may have wanted at one time, but don't seem to be in your future? List them below, and consider how you might let these things go.

WHAT FEELINGS HAVE BEEN BUBBLING UP INSIDE YOU LATELY?

Allow yourself a break from holding everything in and allow those emotions to rise to the surface. Jot any strong feelings down on the bubbles below.

Who are all the people you can trust with these feelings? List them below:

Feelings
are just
visitors.
Let them
come and go.

—MOOJI

YOUR TRUE SELF

IS A TREASURE OF ALL DIVINE VIRTUES.

—MA JAYA

OUR MINDS AND BODIES TEND TO ABSORB OUR SURROUNDINGS. In a
traffic jam, we are an irritable medley of car exhaust, angry horns, and stunted progress. At home, we might be scented candles, classical music, and self-assurance.

The next time you feel worked up or anxious, consider your surroundings and whether they might be a major influence.

SURROUNDINGS WHERE I'M LEAST MYSELF

SURROUNDINGS WHERE I'M MOST MYSELF

DON'T HUNT FOR HAPPINESS. Let happiness come to you in whatever measure or form it wants. Let it be small and truthful rather than big and forced. Maybe it's a sentimental sense of longing for a moment in your past. Maybe it's a feeling of comfort as you snuggle into your favorite spot on the couch. It can be as simple as the zing of recognition when you hear a song you love.

What memory brings you happiness every time you return to it?

What small surprise made your day brighter?

Happiness is not
a matter of intensity
but of balance,
order, rhythm,
and harmony.

—THOMAS MERTON

DON'T LET YOUR MENTAL TO-DO LISTS CROWD OUT MORE MEANINGFUL, LIFE-AFFIRMING THOUGHTS. Free space in your brain for rich ideas and new connections to form.

First, pour your task list onto the page below:

NOW YOU CAN MOVE ON. CONSIDER SOME OF THESE DEEPER, MORE LIFE-AFFIRMING QUESTIONS:

What do you want from life?

What brings you the most happiness?

What have you been meaning to do that you haven't gotten around to?

SCHEDULE YOUR SERENITY. Set a timer on your watch, phone, or laptop. Take a quick, but deserved, pause. Consider your whole self. Unwind your spool of thoughts all the way to their end, then just exist for a few moments with your eyes closed.

Squeeze in one serenity break every day for a week. Hold yourself accountable by scheduling them on the weeklong calendar below.

TIME OF DAY

MONDAY

TUESDAY

WEDNESDAY

THURSDAY

FRIDAY

SATURDAY

SUNDAY

Float

WITHOUT
PURPOSE
OR CARE.

Who are the people you feel most relaxed around? Who
always reminds you to wind down and enjoy life? Add
their names to the petals at the center of this lotus. This
is your support network.

Invite these individuals into your life in any way
possible. Call on them when you need them, be there to
help them when they need it, and tell them how much
they mean to you.

Dear support network:

There are some things you learn best in calm, and some in storm.

—WILLA CATHER

FEELING ANXIOUS OR UNCOMFORTABLE ISN'T ALWAYS A WASTE OF TIME. It has its purpose, and that purpose is to awaken a realization, rouse your inner strength, or even guide you in a healthier direction. Anxiety is sometimes a signal that something isn't right in your life. It can be your body's equivalent of an emergency flare drawing attention to a truth you've been ignoring.

What truth has anxiety forced you to confront:

_____

_____

_____

_____

_____

When has anxiety changed your course?

_____

_____

_____

_____

_____

NEW EXPERIENCES GIVE US A NEW WAY OF LOOKING AT THE WORLD.

Nothing staves off boredom and depression better than adventure, change, and a touch of daring. Surprise yourself today by venturing somewhere new or saying something you never thought you'd have the courage to say. We think we know ourselves, but there is always more to learn.

How can you make today spectacularly different from yesterday?

WAIT FOR A WINNING DAY. Some days will defeat you, others will encourage and reward you, and still others will leave you smack dab in the middle. Where does today fall on that continuum? Circle a number between 1 (unsatisfying) and 10 (incredibly satisfying).

1   2   3   4   5   6   7   8   9   10

If ever the day is unsatisfying, rest assured that there is a more stellar one on the horizon. Describe what makes a day a win:

SCENTS HAVE THE POWER TO UNLOCK OUR DEEPEST MEMORIES AND SHIFT OUR EMOTIONS. A scent can carry us back in time to our childhood, make us feel like we're frolicking in nature, or awaken our senses to help quiet our minds. Vanilla, sage, and lavender are just a few scents with the power to transport us to a calmer frame of mind.

Circle any of the scents below that make you happy or more content.

VANILLA

LEMON

ORANGE

FRESH-CUT GRASS

PEPPERMINT

SAGE

ALMOND

LAVENDER

ROSES

If you haven't found your own favorite scent yet, make a point to experiment with comforting aromas today.

TAKE YOURSELF TOO SERIOUSLY AND EACH DAY WILL FEEL LIKE YOU'RE RUNNING A GAUNTLET. Take today in stride and give yourself as many moments of laughter as possible. Consider some of the funniest moments of this past month and record them below.

Most wonderfully awkward moment:

Major side-splitting, laugh-out-loud moment:

Funniest thing I read, heard, or saw:

A well-developed sense of humor

IS THE POLE THAT ADDS

BALANCE TO YOUR STEPS

AS YOU WALK THE

TIGHTROPE OF LIFE.

—WILLIAM ARTHUR WARD

EXERCISE MAY SEEM LIKE THE OPPOSITE OF CALM, but it can bring you to new levels of inner peace, so just keep moving. It only takes about five minutes of aerobic exercise to start reducing anxiety levels. The more you move during the day, the better you'll feel and sleep at night. Add a 5-10 minute physical break to each day of your week. Consider doing a forest walk, an impromptu dance to your favorite song, yoga, or anything else you enjoy.

	TIME OF DAY	TYPE OF MOVEMENT
Monday		
Tuesday		
Wednesday		
Thursday		
Friday		
Saturday		
Sunday		

Color

IS A POWER
WHICH DIRECTLY
INFLUENCES
THE SOUL.

—WASSILY KANDINSKY

CONSIDER THE WAY THAT COLORS CAN AFFECT YOUR MOOD OR HELP YOU RELAX. With what colors do you surround yourself? Look around your home or survey the clothes in your bedroom closet if you're not sure.

What colors irritate or unsettle you?

How can you add more of the positive colors you like to your life? Where can you create a calming oasis in your home that's rich with these colors?

START AND END YOUR DAY WITH THE
SAME CALMING RITUAL. You'll be surprised
by the way it envelops your day into a complete and
more satisfying bundle. Consider some of these simple
rituals to help you bookend your day:

+ **PLAY A SONG YOU LOVE**

+ **READ A FAVORITE POEM**

+ **TAKE A WALK**

+ **SNUGGLE WITH A PET**

+ **GET INTO A FAVORITE
  YOGA POSE OR STRETCH**

+ **DRINK TEA**

+ **JOURNAL**

Ritual

LULLS OUR FEAR OF DISORDER WITH THE CERTAINTY OF ORDER.

—E. M. BRONER

NATURE IS ALWAYS GOOD THERAPY.

Make a point to lie down in the grass today and stare up at the sky. Find animal shapes in the clouds, let the birds sing to you for a while, and find your place in the scheme of things.

Where do you go to find a connection with nature?

What nature activities have you enjoyed since childhood?

Adopt the pace of nature:

HER SECRET IS PATIENCE.

—RALPH WALDO EMERSON

It is not the mountain we conquer, but ourselves.

—EDMUND HILLARY

WE SPEND TOO MUCH TIME
STANDING IN THE SHADOWS OF
OUR OWN WORRY. Step out of the shadows
today and bask in optimism.

What mountains of worry are looming over you?

How might everything turn out better than you think?

GIVE YOURSELF A GIFT TODAY. Look for beautiful everyday objects or natural objects all around you. Choose one that sparks a feeling of happiness in you and carry it around as a reminder that life is a wonder and you are worth it.

Draw or describe the object you gifted yourself today.

What is wondrous about it?

YOU DON'T HAVE TO BE AN ARTIST TO CREATE A WORK OF ART. Find a form of artistic expression that helps you release your emotions. Number these art forms in order from 1 (art form you'd most enjoy) to 10 (art form you'd least enjoy). Resolve to work one of your top picks into your daily or weekly life.

_____ PAINTING

_____ ORIGAMI

_____ KNITTING

_____ COLORING

_____ DRAWING

_____ WRITING IN A JOURNAL

_____ PLAYING AN INSTRUMENT

_____ DANCING

_____ PHOTOGRAPHY

_____ COOKING

IMAGINE HOW MUCH YOU COULD DO IF YOU STOPPED CRITIQUING YOURSELF ALONG THE WAY. Move beyond any inhibitions you have of yourself as an artist by drawing in the dark. Turn off all the lights or find a dark corner or closet where it's even darker, and go! Let your pencil cruise freely about the page below.

ADOPT A MANTRA TODAY. Here are some calming mantras to consider.

All is well.

What will be will be.

I can handle anything.

One day at a time.

It's all going to be okay.

I don't have to be perfect.

I can only do what I can do.

There's nothing to fear.

I am enough.

Write your favorite mantras on the shapes below. Add any other empowering phrases that feel good when you say them out loud. Read them to yourself at the start of each day. Tap into these words for strength.

MUSIC IS THE SOUL'S COMFORT. Create
or find a playlist of songs that puts your mind at ease. Let
this be the soundtrack for your day.

Songs or artists that relax me:

Songs or artists that energize me:

Ways I can add music to my life:

Feed the soul

USE COLOR TO HELP WITH MINDFUL BREATHING.

Imagine when you inhale that you are breathing in a beautiful ribbon of air. Breathe in all the lightest, brightest colors and imagine that you are absorbing their positive vibes. When you exhale, imagine just the opposite—that you are pushing out all the darkest, most negative vibes with your breath.

Draw the swirls of your breath here. Positivity in; negativity out. Lightness in; darkness out.

How did this work for you? What other techniques do you use for mindful breathing?

ADD PLAY TIME TO YOUR DAY. When you feel the pressure of work and responsibility mounting, schedule time for lighthearted distraction and pointless fun to keep things in perspective.

Send a joke or meme to a good friend, make a playdoh sculpture, or bounce a tennis ball against the wall until you're calm and collected.

Imagine that this is a drawer in your home or office. Draw toys inside of it. Fill it with fun objects that would give you a welcome break.

DEEP MEANING
LIES OFTEN IN
childish play.

—JOHANN FRIEDRICH VON SCHILLER

Gratitude is the fairest blossom which springs from the soul.

—HENRY WARD BEECHER

FIND TIME TO GIVE THANKS TO THE UNIVERSE. No matter how challenging your day may be, making note of the positive aspects of your life keeps you focused on what really matters. Train your brain to do this until it becomes a new habit.

List all the ways you are fortunate below:

1. _____

_____

2. _____

_____

3. _____

_____

4. _____

_____

5. _____

_____

6. _____

_____

7. _____

_____

GO TO YOUR HAPPY PLACE. Literally.
Consider the kinds of destinations that work for you.

What was the best vacation you've ever enjoyed?

What beautiful or peaceful destinations do you hope to
visit someday?

Find an image of a destination that inspires you and
paste it here.

LIGHT IS A MOOD CHANGER. Imbue your home with soft candles that encourage you to slow down and reflect, starry string lights for a hopeful, festive feel, and golden glowing lamps that invite you to read and relax. Illuminate your world and your soul at the same time.

How can you add more sunlight to your life?

What is the brightest and happiest room in your home?

Keep your face to the sun and you will never see the shadows.

—HELEN KELLER

MANY OF US HAVE LEARNED TO VALUE SPEED AND EFFICIENCY OVER QUALITY OF EXPERIENCE. We rush along on the highway of our daily experiences with barely enough time to sneak a glance at the passing scenery. Give yourself permission to slow down today.

I hereby grant myself,

_____,

PRINT NAME

permission to slow down and find the time to be aware of my inner thoughts, needs, and emotions.

Signed,

When was the last time you slowed down and lived in the moment? Describe it and what it did for you.

What role do your cell phone and other electronic
devices play in your life?

In what way, if any, do you want that role to change?

How can you make this plan happen?

Describe your definition of a good work/life balance below.

_____

_____

_____

_____

_____

_____

_____

_____

_____

_____

_____

_____

_____

_____

WHAT ARE YOU HOPING TO GET DONE TODAY? Draw it on the blue half of the circle on the facing page.

WHAT ARE YOU HOPING TO ENJOY TODAY? Draw it on the green half of the circle.

What do you notice about the balance of your day?

_____

_____

_____

_____

_____

ONE WAY TO CHOOSE CALM IS TO
GO "OFF THE GRID." Find a way to make
yourself immune to interruptions today, at least for one
full hour. Record what you did with that time below and
how it felt.

Amount of Time I Spent "Off the Grid" Today:

_____

What I Did:

_____

_____

_____

_____

How It Felt:

_____

_____

_____

_____

FIND
Your Peace

Sleep
IS THE BEST
MEDITATION.

—DALAI LAMA

SLEEP IS A HEALING AND SATISFYING
FORM OF THERAPY. It allows our brains to
roam freely over the landscape of our day so that we can
process what happened and begin to let go.

What is one change you can make to get more , or
deeper, sleep?

When has a dream felt a bit like therapy?

When have you come to a decision about something
after a solid night of sleep?

FILL THIS PAGE WITH ELEMENTS OF HOPE AND PROMISE.

Write down exciting plans you've made for the near or distant future.

_____

_____

_____

_____

Jot down goals that you feel confident you can reach.

1. _____

_____

_____

2. _____

_____

_____

3. _____

_____

_____

Give yourself a well-deserved pat on the back and make note of any recent successes.

What is going really well for you right now?

Read this hopeful page out loud to yourself. Read it again whenever you need a skip in your step.

SUMMON ALL OF YOUR CONFIDENCE WHEN ANXIETY TAKES HOLD. Find that inner core of strength and will it to the surface. Remind yourself that you can handle anything that comes your way.

In what area of your life are you most confident?

Who gives you confidence?

What gives you confidence?

Add or draw a picture of yourself below looking your most confident.

CHANCES ARE, YOU HAVE A DEEP SUPPORT NETWORK. Still, there may be times when you must count on yourself to get through an ordeal or a stressful day. Take time to practice being your own best cheerleader.

Make a list of your best qualities here:

What are some qualities your friends and family would add to this list?

What are some qualities your coworkers would add?

BECAUSE ONE BELIEVES
IN ONESELF, ONE DOESN'T
TRY TO CONVINCE.

BECAUSE ONE IS CONTENT
WITH ONESELF, ONE DOESN'T
NEED OTHERS' APPROVAL.

BECAUSE ONE ACCEPTS
ONESELF, THE WHOLE WORLD
ACCEPTS HIM OR HER.

—LAO TZU

FEAR IS OFTEN AT THE SOURCE OF ANXIETY. Sometimes finding peace means facing our fears. If your emotions seem disproportionate to the situation, look within. Are you afraid to fail? Afraid to be on your own? Afraid of letting someone down?

What type of problem do you tend to blow out of proportion?

What fear is probably lurking behind that problem?

Describe a time when you faced your fears:

Everything you have ever wanted is on the other side of fear.

-GEORGE ADDAIR

IMAGINE THAT YOU ARE VERY OLD AND VERY HAPPY. Imagine that your worst fears were never realized.

How would you feel about the time spent worrying and fearing the worst?

What would matter most now?

Each morning we are born again.

WHAT WE DO TODAY IS WHAT MATTERS MOST.

—BUDDHA

START EACH DAY BY CLEARING OUT THE EMOTIONAL CLUTTER AND MAKING ROOM FOR A NEW BEGINNING. Write down every nagging feeling that is lingering from yesterday or the days that came before it. Fill this page with pesky worries, doubts, angst, problems, bitterness, and stress. Spill them all here.

Scribble out the words in heavy marker or—better yet—tear out the page and rip it to shreds.

START THIS DAY AS IF IT WERE GOING TO BE THE BEST DAY EVER. Challenge yourself to do something bold: Open the window of your house or car and yell a positive, joyful, freeing, or empowering message for all to hear.

Write your "shout-it-to-the-world" message in the center of this window and resolve to begin your day with confidence and hope.

TAKE A VACATION FROM ANXIETY
TODAY. Sail away with the current to gentler waters
and drop anchor until you feel stronger.

What are some of your favorite ways to escape? Circle
any that apply.

✦ READING

✦ CHAT SESSION WITH FRIEND/FAMILY

✦ WATCHING A SHOW/MOVIE

✦ LONG WALK/RUN

✦ LONG DRIVE

✦ YOGA

✦ _____

✦ _____

✦ _____

✦ _____

When has escaping led to a change in perspective?

MAP YOUR DAY ON THE CHART
BELOW. Add points for the highs and lows. Connect
your points with lines. Color in the area of your day.
Notice how the highs are connected to and supported by
the lows.

MORNING   MID-DAY   EVENING

What can you do to ensure even more highpoints tomorrow?

THERE IS MORE TO YOU THAN MOST PEOPLE REALIZE. Don't let other people tell you who you are, and don't let your worries define you.

Write down five words or characteristics that are definitely NOT you:

1. _____

2. _____

3. _____

4. _____

5. _____

Who just doesn't get you?

_____

_____

_____

_____

_____

_____

_____

_____

You are more than one thing. You are many things all at once.

Fill in each stone with a word that truly defines you.

STRESS CAN PUT US ON AN ISLAND OF OUR OWN WORRIES.

When has someone dismissed or downplayed your worries and left you feeling marooned?

Write a letter to your most trusted confidante here. Help them understand how they can support you.

Dear _____ ,

Here are some signs that I'm truly stressed out: _____

_____

_____

_____

_____ .

When I'm ready to talk to you about my worries, I'd really appreciate it if you _____

_____

_____

_____

_____

_____ .

I promise to be there for you in the same way when you need it, so tell me what you need when you're stressed.

Sincerely,

_____

MISTAKES ARE EVIDENCE THAT
YOU'RE TAKING CHANCES AND ARE
TRULY ALIVE. Throw a party for your mistakes
today instead of feeling horrible about them. Write
them on the balloons below and give them the fanfare
they deserve.

Experience is simply the name we give our mistakes.

—OSCAR WILDE

Be light

GIVE AS MUCH AS YOU CAN TO OTHERS, BUT KNOW YOUR OWN PERSONAL LIMIT.

Say no to people when the weight of responsibility is too heavy. Say it without an ounce of guilt or regret. The more you say it, the more comfortable you will be saying it.

Who are you happy to take care of right now?

What added responsibilities would you like to say no to?

WHAT'S YOUR IDEAL BALANCE OF ALONE TIME AND SOCIAL TIME EACH DAY? Fill the circle below to show how much alone time and social time you need in a day. Use one color to represent alone time and one to represent social time.

Being alone isn't something we're all equally comfortable doing. Consider your feelings about spending time alone. Do you avoid it, not mind it, or love it?

If you find yourself overloading your schedule with social events, take a step back to consider whether you're avoiding being alone with a problem. Have you ever run away from dealing with pain, struggle, or self-reflection? Explain.

Alone time can bring unexpected gifts. What has alone time encouraged you to discover/do?

PAUSE TO REFLECT. Writing in a journal or stopping to consider your feelings is the kind of self-care that keeps panic and stress at bay. We all need to vent to stay balanced and happy.

Think back to your youth. How were you taught to vent your feelings? How well does this method work for you now?

What form of venting comes most naturally to you? Circle one or add your own.

ARTISTIC EXPRESSION

JOURNALING

TALKING IT OUT

Practice venting your feelings by journaling. Write a journal entry below:

CHOOSE HOW YOU WANT TO APPROACH YOUR LIFE.

What qualities will you personify? Circle all of the words here that represent life at its best.

Come back to this page anytime and circle these words again and again. Choose them every day and live purposefully. Find comfort knowing that while you may not control the world around you, you do control how you face it.

LIGHTNESS

SELF-DOUBT

SADNESS

HUMOR

JOY

WORRY

BALANCE

ANGST

HOPE

STRESS

HEAVINESS

SELF-CONFIDENCE

The greatest weapon
against stress
is our ability to
choose one thought
over another.

-WILLIAM JAMES